QUANTUM MECHANTICS
MEMOIRS OF A QUARK

BRAD BAUMGARTNER

the operating system digital print//document
QUANTUM MECHANTICS: MEMOIRS OF A QUARK

copyright © 2019 by Brad Baumgartner
edited and designed by ELÆ [Lynne DeSilva-Johnson] with Orchid Tierney
ISBN for print version: 978-1-946031-05-1

is released under a Creative Commons CC-BY-NC-ND (Attribution, Non Commercial, No Derivatives) License: its reproduction is encouraged for those who otherwise could not afford its purchase in the case of academic, personal, and other creative usage from which no profit will accrue.

Complete rules and restrictions are available at:
http://creativecommons.org/licenses/by-nc-nd/3.0/

For additional questions regarding reproduction, quotation, or to request a pdf for review contact operator@theoperatingsystem.org

Print books from The Operating System are distributed to the trade by SPD/Small Press Distribution, with ePub and POD via Ingram, with production by Spencer Printing, in Honesdale, PA, in the USA. Digital books are available directly from the OS, direct from authors, via DIY pamplet printing, and/or POD.

This text was set in Steelworks Vintage, Europa-Light, Gill Sans, Minion, Cambria Math, Courier New, and OCR-A Standard.

Cover Art uses an image from the series "Collected Objects & the Dead Birds I Did Not Carry Home," by Heidi Reszies. [Cover Image Description: Mixed media collage using torn pieces of paper in blue, gray, and red tones, and title of the book in yellow and blue.]

The Operating System is a member of the **Radical Open Access Collective**, a community of scholar-led, not-for-profit presses, journals and other open access projects. Now consisting of 40 members, we promote a progressive vision for open publishing in the humanities and social sciences. Learn more at: http://radicaloa.disruptivemedia.org.uk/about/

Your donation makes our publications, platform and programs possible! We <3 You.
http://www.theoperatingsystem.org/subscribe-join/

the operating system
www.theoperatingsystem.org

QUANTUM MECHANTICS
MEMOIRS OF A QUARK

CONTENTS

Foreword

1. Crypto-Meontology   1

2. Gorgias the Twin Star   13

3. Uncertaintied   23

4. Subatomic Scapulae   37

5. Energy of the Seventh Heart   45

FOREWORD

The quantum world, like the mystical, is anonymous, aporetic, hidden.

In order to view the weirdness of the micro-scop(ophil)ic (scopophilia from Greek σκοπέω *skopeō*, "look to, examine") quantum world—a world, no less, filled with particles popping *ex nihilo*; of what Einstein once famously called "spooky action at a distance"—this short collection takes as its subject matter a myriad of interfacings—quantum physics, mysticism, cryptography, impersonality, and meontology, to name a few. As such, the text operationalizes a parthenogenetic-pathetic fallacy, attributing the ultimate (first, final, last, and never was) paroxyic paradox upon the quarkic Word (Logos): an impersonal knowledge-without-a-bearer, that is to say, a knowing which knows nothing as voiced through the unbeginning Nemo-clature of an eternal, hopping quant-Al(l)ity.

Playfully rigorous and rigorously playful, *Quantum Mechantics* thus experimentally indexes a form of ludic hopping (hop, from Old English hoppian "to spring, leap; to dance; to limp"), that is, a sha(Brah)manic "dances with words" in which the Word itself spontaneously leaps vis-à-vis what we might call a 'tripling manas' (from Sanscrit, manas means "mind"): *manically, maniacally*, in quanto-*manicular* gestures, pointing back at themselves—as text objects and speech acts—in order to curate a series of significations that complicate, negate, and ultimately reinstate their own function as signifiers.

These text objects perform as the quantum world does: boggling "the mind" and loosening their prowess, we discover a subatomic, translucent poetry-without-us.

Brad Baumgartner
July 14, 2018

For Our Dreams and Our Dances

"If quarks could talk,
All'd start to walk."
— radion

"If quarks could write,
All'd be all right."
— dilaton

ONE
CRYPTO-MEONTOLOGY

(\(n\))   (\(l\)) (\(m_l\))   (\(m_s\))

///

what is
hidden and
what is   hiding

      hide-bearing and
      borne of a crisp
      mountain egg

all the blowing
rain inside the canal
an ear with wings

      protons packing heat
      Heads on Fire
      strewn about, dance carved

///

embracing DUST
called into a whimper
shorted and circuits
dreaded to the death

///

is not is, not is: is not

///

collectively; no eyes to see, no
rain upon the gait, two legs
don't strive to walk away, the
dead collect their rent

///

need not exist in faces
unending fade to dream
unkempt within the wisp
hides nowhere to blame

///

b e g i n n i n g   b e n i g n n i n g   b e N I N E i n g

///

deaf ton a world a stray
detonate detonate ton gate
      worlds astray
straight as a bone: losing
the way,
a
      GREAT COLD MIST
STARRY

///

froZEN

///

NON-hate

///

A + A → ØA + A → ØA + A → ØA + A → ØA + A → ØA + A → ØA + A → Ø A + A → ØA + A → ØA + A → ØA + A → ØA + A → ØA + A → ØA + A → ØA + A → ØA + A → ØA + A → ØNULLA + A → ØA + A → ØA + A → ØA + A → Ø A + A → ØA + A → ØA + A → ØA + A → ØA + A → ØA + A → ØA + A → ØA + A → Ø A + A → ØA + A → ØA + A → ØA + A → ØA + A → ØA + A → ØA + A → ØA + A → ØA + A → Ø A + A → ØA + A → ØA + A → ØA + A → ØA + A → ØA + A → ØA + A → ØA + A → ØA + A → Ø A + A → ØA + A → ØA + A → ØNULLA + A → ØA + A → ØA + A → ØA + A → ØA + A → ØA + A → ØA + A → ØA + A → ØA + A → ØA + A → Ø A + A → ØA + A → ØA + A → ØA + A → ØA + A → ØA + A → ØA + A → ØA + A → ØA + A → ØA + A → ØA + A → ØA + A → ØA + A → ØA + A → Ø A + A → ØA + A → ØA + A → ØA + A → ØA + A → ØA + A → ØA + A → ØA + A → Ø A + A → ØA + A → ØA + A → ØA + A → ØA + A → ØA + A → ØA + A → ØA + A → ØA + A → Ø A + A → ØA + A → ØA + A → ØA + A → ØA + A → ØA + A → ØA + A → ØA + A → Ø A + A → ØA + A → Ø A + A → ØA + A → ØBULLSEYEA + A → ØA + A → ØA + A → ØA + A → ØA + A → ØA + A → ØA + A → ØA + A → ØA + A → ØA + A → ØA + A → Ø A + A → ØA + A → ØA + A → ØA + A → ØA + A → ØA + A → ØA + A → ØA + A → Ø A + A → ØA + A → ØA + A → ØA + A → ØNULLA + A → ØA + A → ØA + A → ØA + A → ØA + A → ØA + A → ØA + A → ØA + A → ØA + A → ØA + A → ØA + A → ØA + A → Ø A + A → ØA + A → ØA + A → ØNULLA + A → ØA + A → ØA + A → ØA + A → ØA + A → Ø A + A → ØA + A → ØA + A → ØA + A → ØA + A → ØA + A → ØA + A → ØA + A → ØA + A → ØA + A → Ø A + A → ØA + A → ØA + A → ØA + A → ØA + A → ØA + A → ØA + A → ØA + A → ØA + A → Ø A + A → ØA + A → ØA + A → ØA + A → ØNULLA + A → ØA + A → ØA + A → ØA + A → ØA + A → Ø A + A → ØA + A → ØA + A → ØA + A → ØA + A → ØA + A → ØA + A → ØA + A → ØA + A → ØA + A → ØA + A → ØA + A → Ø A + A → ØA + A → ØA + A → ØA + A → ØA + A → ØA + A → ØA + A → ØA + A → ØA + A → ØA + A → Ø A + A → ØØA + A → ØA + A → ØA + A → ØØØØØØØØØØØSIGH

///

CREATION OPERATOR ((((((((((((((((((((((((((((((_BOSONIC PERPETRATOR_))))))))))))))))
ANNIHILATIONOPERATOR <<<<<<<<<<CREATIONTRAITOR>>>>>>>>>>>

///

ENTER HERE (NO/W-HERE)

///

•⁻ ⁻••• ••• • ⁻• ⁻•⁻• •

///

code counter / the pink moon
echo echo / strewn / love touch
found out / in / out / absence
silence
ace dance / lance
      co-lapsed

///

collapse: wave function

///

quagmire throne shambled
bemoan—moon shaft dormant
          HONEY
combed caned calmed collected

///

forgetting the mendicant scion

///

a current,   a wave
hums are numbers
numbing, thoracic
    spiral wanderers
           kundalini goat hoppers
  cone portal, scenic
  frock, alone lone a

///

Sssscum threader, meat of
Flash drill selling
Nothing nothing no
Thong sex wheelhouse
Double fisted thirst
Thruster manhole wash
House hose panties
Cash monkey skilled
Trinkets dash pole ritual
Phantom harvest

///

blood pummeling

///

sampling nimble forays

///

axiomatrix

///

being towards breadth

///

bachelor throng evental
tubular tributary
harvest rampant
weaklings milking
a welkin lozenge

///

physic pyrrhic
dominatrix

///

empty ramblers
scraping barrier
hounds tooth scant

///

TNT chattering

///

pointless dawn
down
    sown
        soundlessly

///

Peonic Pessimism

///

cunning tunnel
    t o n g u i n g
        f u n n e l

///

equations eek quell quasars

///
====================

///

along the watchsours
after the solid spinals
into the whitening slender
wyrding sly mother tongues
slick, stone sawing eyes

///

regurgigyrating
                    the requisite
            SPLENDOR SOLIS

///

testimanicular throneshawl / tossed erroneous

///

wings
ARCH angles
dreams in witch houses /
sire sirens dire dowel rockets
brewed course erogenous genome
fountain bleu mocked emoticon snatched

///

ecotutorial equatorpor

///

sloth mongering . . . Mongol cou   nt   do w n . . .

///

ironlung lion in Zion

///

mango marinade Dada exhume exude attribute deny powered hopeless bouncing harmonies

///

anagogic phantasy / the lone drone / mystic marriage carriage

TWO
GORGIAS THE TWIN STAR

EMPTY SPACE FLUCTUATIONSSSSSSSS

///

UUUnitarity unquenchanable uniterated interminable squandered scoundrellian UUUnitarity unquenchanable uniterated interminable squandered scoundrellian UUUnitarity unquenchanable uniterated interminable squandered scoundrellian UUUnitarity unquenchanable uniterated interminable squandered scoundrellian UUUnitarity unquenchanable uniterated interminable squandered scoundrellian UUUnitarity unquenchanable uniterated interminable squandered scoundrellian UUUnitarity unquenchanable uniterated interminable squandered scoundrellian UUUnitarity unquenchanable uniterated interminable squandered scoundrellian UUUnitarity unquenchanable uniterated interminable squandered scoundrellian UUUnitarity unquenchanable uniterated interminable squandered scoundrellian UUUnitarity unquenchanable uniterated interminable squandered scoundrellian **BLACK HOWL HOLE** UUUnitarity unquenchanable uniterated interminable squandered scoundrellian UUUnitarity unquenchanable uniterated interminable squandered scoundrellian UUUnitarity unquenchanable uniterated interminable squandered scoundrellian UUUnitarity unquenchanable uniterated interminable squandered scoundrellian UUUnitarity unquenchanable uniterated interminable squandered scoundrellian UUUnitarity unquenchanable uniterated interminable squandered scoundrellian UUUnitarity **777**

///

spontanAEONS segregation

///

enventitude of the Gorgias Star, the twin the twin
//

is as above
so be LOW

//

quantic quark scheme,
the unrivaled NEMOclature:
thirst-thrift-throttle-moaning

//

GORGIas, NON and on and on and NON and on and on
and NON and on and on and NON

//

siphoned stately stalemate,
the AIN SOPHist

///

AND on AND   on AND on   AND on AND
        on AND on   (GORGIAS the NAYSAYER)
non AND non   NON NON   non AND non
        NON NON   ~~(GORGIAS the NAYSAYER)~~
AND on AND   on AND on   AND on AND
        on AND on   (GORGIAS the NAYSAYER)
non AND non   NON NON   non AND non
        NON NON   ~~(GORGIAS the NAYSAYER)~~

///

Pro-seed the question with the no answerve, a light

delight from the # HILLTOP MØØN ... so many quarks in the non-native swirls.

///

The nay-Sayer

///

neigh neigh!
Neti Neti!!!!!

///

quark-tronic sine enhancer

///

pointed at the *pointing*

///

Call of the Ariadne Diamond
    diamonded
        diamondhead
            diametrically dead
                dialogue of the deaf

///

mouth full of quarks and so quirky are the nightin-
gales that sing so many nights a year,
full of flows,
lost in flowers,
there are no bees,
but only wings

in a prairie, a prairie with no sand
HARK!, the quark that speaks its
own rhythms, its own field of
impossibility

///

the inhuman swirl of a hand
less dawn

///

      c   ol ors
         rainbow
    cut   onus

///

Crown of ubiquitY
Palindrome hammeR
Stark negative ioniC
Sphere spears at thE
Gates of MIRE, tO
Go and never go, bE
Ing there and neveR
Not not beinG

///

jumble thimble soundless and the mercy given

thriving not at the juncture of a spontaneous gift

///

blood coddled moor scraps
    bloated flood goat
        ionic spheroid columning

///

phantasmagnomic

///

squirm Cancerian squire mustering

///

Cathedral breath

///

wrath caulked simian noumenclature

///

rattle snake lube feud /
twisted urethra ether

///

maniFaust density

///

HARDENING LUMPS
FACING **EITHER/OR**
ALING ALONG FRONTIERED LAMBASTS

///

grain of Samadhi

///

malefic throne squabbling

///

shout toothed Mongol hammer

///

weight of dunes
scrapped
delighted

///

jumping:::thrown:::sipping
mires:::begotten:::gooned///flooded///

///

m
    a
     r
     o
      o
      n
         e
      d   is-
lander

THREE
UNCERTAINTIED

metempsychosis s tar lover without a hand and two eyes spa treating engendered androgynocopia allotting mindmasses dark cathedral hive money 555 can spun winters the goop of eye masks furious lighthouses and mindaltering smugs 999 frowncosts dander haired monsters globule drafts with sandstorms bereft of matching harnesses 444 black clap plank stamp 111 white white white thespian pinhead needle coin 222 shroud of false pneumatic materialism stand moaning away swatting at life guarding seven toad mouths months moths THOTH 777 frowned upon found up on hills and magnet maggot stones and winter haired ghosts in clay 777 dark haired winter 777 short style crisper 777 re member the lodge no windows severed heads handing hanging baskets dangling ganglion cysts and stones breaking bones spinal cords errant drafts kings and kindly queen bees never coddling workers play platitudes attitudinally whimpering strange Beloit sounds cattle prodding at a lover's genuine vein glorious metonymphomania

///

hallowed hollowed shallowed swallowed
haloed holographic holiverse
lowered lowed loved load
platypus proclamation pigpen pen pal
subterfuge surge surreptitious slinkiness
demiurge mirth myth minus might

///

tardigradient splendevour king
^^^^^mountain ^^^^^surprise
castling ecologico-multiversal
quantum biorhythmic surmise

///

entangled state, finagled slate, bilateral straight, entombs
                                      remain

///

UNiCoRNS BLaCK HoLe-HoWLiNG

///

chupacabra floriographyy
harmonium majored in D
onslaught: three minus three
zero zero zero zero zero zero zero zero zero zero zero zero zero
zero zero zero zero zer ze z

///

necrot, tribes, two thimbles, a mime—
glory of Olde, two germs, a slate6
gathering protonic oozing a life6
mires within mires blot blot blotted6

///

COLDWARMBUZZBUZZSLATEDzzzBONES

///

Bantam weights still flurry ghosts
Shot goat down haven hell maven
Silly cowlick drowned out ant dwarf

Superlative hammered mirrorstar

///

BARDO APOCOLYPSE

///

screamed night of wrought
wrought   wrought
naught naught night naught
naught naught naught breathing
s l o w i n g *nulla*

///

$$^{23}_{12}Mg \rightarrow {}^{23}_{11}Na + e{++}\; ve$$

///

beta decaying magnet wrench wrought wench stench
saundered seventh gate to
ALIENESQUE BIDET

///

trigo(g)nometry immaculate incarnate insolate
inconsolable siphon scion

///

puzzlegut mercenary

///

voodoo lust machine
saw-swallowing
the shallow sheen

///

        ABRACADAVER
        ABRACADAVE
        ABRACADAV
        ABRACADA
        ABRACAD
        ABRACA
        ABRAC
        ABRA
        ABR
        AB
        A

578421

                                                    2
                                          4875
                                                    1

///

eterno-nau(gh)tical sea faring whisper saunas cradle cradled cradling /// chalked up, coughing up chakras

///

4, 6, 10, 12, 16, 96
    144

                1000
                96
                16
                12
                10
                6
                4

                                144,000

///

quanta ... soul shepherd apparatus
star striking amulet needle throne
needling kneading need king
kind kingly unknown dust tripling

///

8191

///

[shown sheen shifter true truth seek] [never knew new never known un—] [capture cultured] [wound womb Wombyn] [vortex cradle] [mold break delirium] [gaze grazed hue mountain]

///

non-soliloquizzically

///

subatomic galactation

///

curdled blood moor of imprecise graftification scanning

///

the blistered squid of hammered lupine modulation

///

double-vision cyclopean blindness
closing in /// dox deus ex machina
a blind birth /// double bind hearth

///

float on the sky
mire maze modeling
+ _____ = em**bold**ening
    modal   ring
sphere center / shape shift / erroneous erogenous
            A<small>NDROGYN</small>E   w (h) i s p e r s

///

stun gaze mirror zapped

///

soporific sophomoric juvenilia

///

   bloodhive scallywag
THOUGHTSEED
slender – slighted – begotten

///

frothmire mirthmachine

///

cold scold sarcophagi stitch stench

///

at the mountains of Mithras

///

campy internment discernment

///

in thrown king merry sheep lead way out down town sleep))((two sorry formaldejekyllandhyde

///

Bardo soused pond delirium quacked quake Melquíades

///

        S
        O
        L
        I
        D
        -
        M
        A
        S
        S
        -
        P
        O
        U
        N
        D
        -
        O
        U
        T
        -

C
O
R
I
N
T
H
I
A
N
-
T
H
R
O
N
E
-
W
O
U
N
D

///

SCOUR SCORCHED DESTROY DARLING DOPPLEGANGER MINIATURE STOUT MONGER WARRIOR QUEER WANTON LOG THROPE FINAGLE GANGLION CYSTEMIC FEATURE FUTURE BEARER WHISPER KING SOLOMAN MYSTIC WOMAN FUSED BELABORED MOTHER WORN WOMB PESSIMUS MASS MAXIMUS SOUR GRIMACE EARBUD SCARSWORD SHADOW LOVE VEHEMENT GAIL FORCE ROMPER WANING MOONSORROW QUALUDE MONK VESPER HILL HOLOGRAM NEVER POTTED WHITHERING SOULTREE SULTRY FRIZZLE MAP YES FROTHING GOAT FIEND USE HER PENDULUM LUDIC MASTER RUNE /<u>ONE</u>/ **in the eloping sphere**

AN ATOM—
through the wind
through the trees
through the mountain
in the wisps
throttled throat-bearer
bouncing attack scorer
threaded stars
beings balk
under the universe
swallowing the drifters

///

square root of Zeno

///

NEMO NEMO NEMO NEMO NEMO NEMO NEMO NEMO NEMO NEMO
NEMO NEMO
NEMO NEMO NEMO NEMO NEMO NEMO NEMO NEMO NEMO
NEMO NEMO
NEMO NEMO NEMO NEMO NEMO NEMO NEMO NEMO NEMO
NEMO NEMO
NEMO NEMO NEMO NEMO NEMO NEMO NEMO NEMO NEMO
NEMO NEMO
NEMO NEMO NEMO NEMO NEMO NEMO NEMO NEMO NEMO
NEMO NEMO
NEMO NEMO NEMO NEMO NEMO NEMO NEMO NEMO NEMO
NEMO NEMO
NEMO NEMO NEMO NEMO NEMO NEMO NEMO NEMO NEMO
NEMO NEMO
YELLOW YELLOW YELLOW DEMON YELLOW YELLOW YELLOW RASPY
YELLOW
NEMO NEMO NEMO NEMO NEMO NEMO NEMO NEMO NEMO NEMO

NEMO NEMO
NEMO NEMO NEMO NEMO NEMO NEMO NEMO NEMO NEMO
NEMO NEMO
NEMO NEMO NEMO NEMO NEMO NEMO NEMO NEMO NEMO
NEMO NEMO
NEMO NEMO NEMO NEMO NEMO NEMO NEMO NEMO NEMO
NEMO NEMO
NEMO NEMO NEMO NEMO NEMO NEMO NEMO NEMO NEMO
NEMO NEMO
NEMO NEMO NEMO NEMO NEMO NEMO NEMO NEMO NEMO
NEMO NEMO
NEMO NEMO NEMO NEMO NEMO NEMO NEMO NEMO NEMO
NEMO NEMO

FOUR
SUBATOMIC SCAPULAE

arcana with the flowering feet
      flowered, hot, tempting
undeveloped morsel of strange undulating glowing
familiar, toadish, goop, tomfool airy
      wary of a dead man
mean, median, mode of inexistence

///

leucine, square hammered
nothing loch[ness]ed, locked and loaded
nested buttered catawampus thrones
mustered up into the nebulousness
    → ←
two throttled moats await its
    stationary state

///

EnVoEtRhYiTnHgI NcGhAaLnWgAeYsS

///

wrapped around the crimson fork
a love touch mallard bark harking
same life no life longing bask masking
twin pitch monster shadow lurk mongering
harness touch and wrinkled feet frothing
weep marigold weep at the shop slaughter

///

gamma ray

        mary maga
halographic projection
        Mary Magdelenocene

///

Operaxiomatic lambasted night drawer of the LIGHT

///

septic moon skin

///

adoration alcove
all-laughing aluminum
agoraphobic anagnorisis

///

bowing to the crow in the mane

///

postulate prostrate inundate
decreate excruciate exhume thelemite
gyrate excoriate ex eye ~~ex eye~~ saw

///

lycanthropenninsula

///

match amber halcyon CYCLONOMORPHEME
tenebrous tedium shower haven mass
squat ton ten brick scalding thott jonesing

///

SQUIRE OF MIRTH
MYTHOS MULE
WORKING HORSE

///

twiddling the fire gate

///

microdiamonds
jealously
connect the grin
of gravity

///

oblate obstinacyclone

///

dēofol mæg caru

///

MANY WORLDS
                            any whirls

                                        w
                                  idth in
                                        w
                                  hich

walls within
walls
without walls

///

    |S| |T| |R| |I| |N|
                |G| |S|

///

C (oddled) fruit
C entered [heresy] shears
O verheard (hearse) {heart} =
O VERHEAT

///

horseplay rattle tail

///

spectroscopy of the excited state
<u>ELECTROHERESY OF THE ECSTATIC STATE</u>

///

collapsible bilocation plug

///

GODHEAD MACHINIC DESIRE COUNTER—
NARRATING ABYSSAL HARMONY

///

saints
saints upon
saints upon saints
saints upon saints upon
saints upon saints upon saints
saints upon saints upon saints upon
saints upon saints upon saints upon saints
saints upon saints upon saints upon saints upon
saints upon saints upon saints upon saints upon saints
upon
upon

upon
upon
upon

FIVE
ENERGY OF THE SEVENTH HEART

attitude of aptitude, uncanny
seventh day of yes-aways, many
drawing straws, token of life
a crux of four/four/four/four to eight
shadows showing seven silver cords

///

coquette, rigmarole, seven beaches, seventy-seven
toads /// principally uncertain, uncertainty principled,
unannounced electronicity, protonic, unveiled ///
rivaled, scavenged, avenged, savaged /// interact,
motioned, scion /// Q/U/A/N/T/I/Z/A/T/I/O/N/ /// auto-
mythopoietic ionization

///

ενέργεια ενέργεια ενέργεια ενέργεια ενέργεια ενέργεια
    ενέργεια ενέργεια ενέργεια ενέργεια ενέργεια
        ενέργεια ενέργεια ενέργεια ενέργεια
      ενέργεια ενέργεια ενέργεια
        ενέργεια ενέργεια
          θερμότητα

///

soul	sole	soul		sin sunder
helical	helical		helium	musk
sun spatter	sun splatter	moon winter		planter

                                        soul helical sun splatter

///

entomb enthrone eunuch enough

///

sssssss eeeeeee vvvvvvv eeeeeee nnnnnnn

///

ssssss iiiiii xxxxxx

///

= = = = =

///

four four four four

///

TRINITY

///

dual/ity

///

... 1 ...

///

ALONE / ALL ONE   . . .   all none noetic node
nun non null all alone non one   ...

///

Christic sun splatter
paridisical harmonium

ex-harlot pneumatica
because a whisper
two thrones and a live
mealworm tree

///

GLEAN-GLEAMING IN THE LIGHT

///

blood championing = karmic love st ain
                                  ®

///

All
      winter wrapped up in
June bugs

///

swallowing the rAIN SOPHistry

///

a lightspeed history of hystericylindricalico fecundo-
felines

///

paint in the light
sky of the dust
darkening Shah
palindrome harness
           Anna

///

777 777 777

///

abiogenetic flâneury
alibi of genetic fallacy
all genuflectic funerary

///

paw tiger into the mute
stream helm hold—help
seven slick winter shards

///

137.50777

///

flower skill
skulls OM
glide glib gris
Thoth daylight

///

filial lyme light, a
future-bearer, scowled
habituation etherized
uni chord nodes of
prayer, vacuums terra
per-forming Love

///

bloated corona
       sol sphere EYE

                        cyclopean cornea
kissing the sky

///

_crucible crucifixing full fine time trough____
ENOUGH naughting KNIGHT time travesties

///

elongated in the neon mud

///

casket brain daughter

///

imp-ersonal con-nouns

///

algebraic onto-egalitarian rainbow drifting

///

radical Aum saga

///

to infinitize / the be-yonder

///

mereo(ntotheo)logical nihilism

///

post-laboratory alien nation

///

scintillated miasmic spelunking
///

machinicicles

///

entropic ordering of the Golden Fawn / invisible speculum of the mourning dawn

///

Aleph
Alpha
All pha

///

FFFIIIRRREEE

///

Fuego / father / pha-air

///

Descending into nostrilism

///

Open pathway eventualism

///

Cosmicist 777 notary republic

///

AsIoNph

///

Sol sphere/
Soul spear/
Soled here/
Sol-are life

///

24

///

galactation..milking planet..descending phallus..hidden clown..internal dimensions..cosmic laws..absolute infinite..ascending Sol

///

Chri-stick rune splendor

///

physical worlds / five five five five five / gardening Eden / sense and non-scents / above /below / protoplasmic / light / vibration / breaking barriers / enticed by light/ fallen in LOVE

///

Seven chvrches UUUUUUUnitarian

///

Om Mega Therion
    ALL
    All
    aLL
        WORD

AFTER-WORDS

AN UNENDING HEART-FOUNTAIN OF COLLABORATIVE OPENNESS
A CONVERSATION WITH BRAD BAUMGARTNER

Greetings comrade! Thank you for talking to us about your process today! Can you introduce yourself, in a way that you would choose?

Hi, I'm Brad. Thank you for the opportunity to talk a little bit about this text!

Why are you a poet/writer/artist?

That's a good question. Maybe I can speak to that more in some of the answers below.

When did you decide you were a poet/writer/artist (and/or: do you feel comfortable calling yourself a poet/writer/artist, what other titles or affiliations do you prefer/feel are more accurate)?

In a certain way, I'm always a bit leery of calling myself anything (for often when one calls oneself something it is actually quite the opposite, i.e. in the sense of sincerity, etc. once expressed by Jean-Paul Sartre in his meditation on "bad faith" in Part One of *Being and Nothingness*). However, being that I've already breached that rule by naming it, I might was well just say it, right? Hah! And writing bios is a part of the writerly life, anyways.

So, yea, I am a writer who is drawn mostly to the genres of poetry, experimental writing, and critical theory—not necessarily in that order, though, and perhaps more in the sense of a kind of theory that is a poetry and a poetry that is a kind of theory (from the Greek theōrein "to consider, speculate, look at").

What's a "poet" (or "writer" or "artist") anyway?

This is a difficult question and the answer is likely different for everyone. Ultimately, though, I am colorfully drawn to Wassily Kandinsky's definition of the artist. Like Kandinsky, I think that at its root the role of the artist is aligned with the *spiritual essence of art*: "If the emotional power of the artist can overwhelm the 'how?' and can give free scope to his finer feelings, then art is on the crest of the road by which she will not fail later on to find the 'what' she has lost, the 'what' which will show the way to the spiritual food of the newly awakened spiritual life. This 'what?' will no longer be the material, objective 'what' of the former period, but the internal truth of art, the soul without which the body (i.e. the 'how') can never be healthy, whether in an individual or in a whole people. [...] This 'what' is the internal truth which only art can divine, which only art can express by those means of expression which are hers alone." (*Concerning the Spiritual in Art,* trans. M. T. H. Sadler [New York: Dover, 1977], 9.)

What do you see as your cultural and social role (in the literary / artistic / creative community and beyond)?

By and large, the general theme of rejected submissions I tend to get is that it is either too poetic to be theory or too theoretical to be poetry. I am quite alright with that, actually, as it means the work is kind of hovering in this third, indistinct space. And being that rejections are a part of the game, it is a pretty fair critique. One of the things I am interested in, creation-wise, is what Nicholas of Cusa once termed a 'coincidentia oppositorum' or "coincidence of opposites," where two opposing things come together as one. So perhaps my cultural/social role, if anything, might be to curate the conditions of possibility, or prop open the door, so to speak, for that coincidence to potentially happen in a readership of some kind.

Did you envision this collection as a collection or understand your process as writing or making specifically around a theme while the poems themselves were being written / the work was being made? How or how not?

As I mention in the brief Foreword to the chapbook, essentially the text operationalizes a parthenogenetic-pathetic fallacy, attributing the ultimate (first, final, last, and never was) paroxyic paradox upon the quarkic Word (Logos). It seeks an impersonal knowledge-without-a-bearer, that is to say a knowing which knows nothing as voiced through the unbeginning Nemo-clature of an eternal, hopping quant-Al(l)ity.

What formal structures or other constrictive practices (if any) do you use in the creation of your work? Have certain teachers or instructive environments, or readings/writings/work of other creative people informed the way you work/write?

During the past several years, I've had a growing interest in several different but interrelated topics, including theoretical physics, the microbiome, artificial intelligence, the non-human—in these sorts of interdisciplinary musings is where I tend to feel most at home these days.

Speaking of monikers, what does your title represent? How was it generated? Talk about the way you titled the book, and how your process of naming (individual pieces, sections, etc) influences you and/or colors your work specifically.

It's a silly title. But it is also indexical to what the text is "doing," which is this sort of interpretive shamanic dance, pointing at itself, saying, "Look at me, if you can (because I'm slippery), but when you do don't take me too seriously; but also do take me seriously, if you can (because I want you to hold me tightly)." I will talk a little more about that below.

What does this particular work represent to you as indicative of your method/creative practice? your history? your mission/intentions/hopes/plans?

In sum, I suppose this text could be 2 or 2000 pages—the length is sort of arbitrary. It could go on forever or stop before it even started. Though one could lodge critiques of anthropomorphism, etc. this text is more of an inhuman poetico-archeology of sorts, or a quantum auto-ethnography done by the quark itself, which is really neither here nor there—more nowhere than anywhere, but always everywhere.

What does this book DO (as much as what it says or contains)?

Without speaking too much for the quark itself, one of the things that this text might aim to achieve is to curate a relation-ship (or a vehic(cup)ular salut!-ation) between the reader and the non-human world—i.e., the quantum world—wherein the readers' own eyes become the effervescing vehicle for a kind of transformation, whether mystical or otherwise. That is an inherently paradoxical statement, however. For if the text objects in the book do in fact perform as the quantum world does, existing/not existing as boggling and indeterminate, then essentially there is nothing to discover other than what we might call a subatomic, quantum 'poetry-without-us'—yet, it is one that paradoxically exists only when observed or read.

On that note, I wonder, too, if all poetic texts/readerships are part of this quantum entanglement.

What would be the best possible outcome for this book? What might it do in the world, and how will its presence as an object facilitate your creative role in your community and beyond? What are your hopes for this book, and for your practice?

That's hard to say, and even harder not to, but if I were to venture a guess, I'd put it something like this: I am always a little suspect of the word "hope" in any capacity, because sometimes, even with the best intentions, it often sets us up for failure via communal- or self-sabotage. When it comes down to it, then, I typically prefer the word courage over hope.

For instance, in the sense of Nietzschean 'amor fati' (or "love of fate"), an idea I put a lot of stock into, essentially nothing is any more important than anything else; that is to say that everything that happens is as it is, not as it should be, because it always already is as it should be. This is a complex idea, but coincidentally it is perhaps best expressed in modern pop cultural parlance via the "It be like that sometimes" meme. And it definitely "be like that" a lot. So we might as well dance with it while it is, which is also to say that in that very dancing, which may be clumsy, erroneous, even a complete failure, that we courageously open ourselves up completely to a kind of beautiful non-dancing, i.e. the potentiality of it simultaneously not being like that. And, in that very dancing, which is also a form of reading, we'll quirkily/quarkily bounce around like the quantum ballerinas and magicians we already are—always and forever.

Let's talk a little bit about the role of poetics and creative community in social activism, in particular in what I call "Civil Rights 2.0," which has remained immediately present all around us in the time leading up to this series' publication. I'd be curious to hear some thoughts on the challenges we face in speaking and publishing across lines of race, age, privilege, social/cultural background, and sexuality within the community, vs. the dangers of remaining and producing in isolated "silos."

Ultimately, I'm all for para-academic mediums, creative outlets, publishing methods, anonymous texts, etc. that foster an open exchange of/for ideas. Our present day socio-political climate being what it is, it especially important to curate venues for enacting a sense of community among people of diverse backgrounds and perspective—a community, no less, that is unfettered by oppressive hegemonic forces; a community that feels like being at a poetry reading with other like-minded poets and not like a contrived 'graduation ceremony' of some sort. In short: the role of poetics serves as a meta-/physical nod of the head or a wink at someone you think is cool, and they think you are, too.

It's a community not just with other humans but also with non-humans—whether they be non-human animals, our quantum friends, mermaids, artificial intelligence, (which we will undoubtedly see within the next decade or two, and may actually have been here all along, who knows!), etc. On the latter, we may not be able to foresee that future just yet—or ever, for that matter—but we may be able to meet it with the courage of open hearts. Perhaps what we need is a very particular kind of collective commune-(ent)ity that seeks to grow itself in and by love. In this way, I'd go so far as to call it a kind of apophatic networking, or group of individuals communing by their mystical knowing-nothing, which, to follow the Beguine mystic Marguerite Porete, gives us everything! So in face of the challenges mentioned above, we find an unending heart-fountain of collaborative openness, the immanent pulsing of radical human freedom.

ABOUT THE AUTHOR

BRAD BAUMGARTNER is a writer, theorist, and Assistant Teaching Professor of English at Penn State. Recent creative work has appeared in *Burning House Press, Tarpaulin Sky Magazine, X Ray Literary Magazine, Vestiges*, and others. Current projects include *Weird Mysticism*, a scholarly monograph, and several creative projects including a hybrid work entitled *Stylinaut*, which was shortlisted for the 2019 Tarpaulin Sky Book Award, and a play called *the -tempered mid·riff*.

ABOUT THE COVER ART:

The Operating System 2019 chapbooks, in both digital and print, feature art from Heidi Reszies. The work is from a series entitled "Collected Objects & the Dead Birds I Did Not Carry Home," which are mixed media collages with encaustic on 8 x 8 wood panel, made in 2018.

Heidi writes: "This series explores objects/fragments of material culture--how objects occupy space, and my relationship to them or to their absence."

ABOUT THE ARTIST:

Heidi Reszies is a poet/transdisciplinary artist living in Richmond, Virginia. Her visual art is included in the National Museum of Women in the Arts CLARA Database of Women Artists. She teaches letterpress printing at the Virginia Commonwealth University School of the Arts, and is the creator/curator of Artifact Press. Her poetry collection titled *Illusory Borders* is forthcoming from The Operating System in 2019, and now available for pre-order. Her collection titled *Of Water & Other Soft Constructions* was selected by Samiya Bashir as the winner of the Anhinga Press 2018 Robert Dana Prize for Poetry (forthcoming in 2019).

Find her at heidireszies.com

WHY PRINT:DOCUMENT?
(AND WHAT DOES THIS MEAN FOR DIGITAL MEDIA?)

The Operating System has traditionally used the language "print:document" to differentiate from the book-object as part of our mission to distinguish the act of documentation-in-book-FORM from the act of publishing as a backwards-facing replication of the book's agentive *role* as it may have appeared the last several centuries of its history. Ultimately, we approach the book as TECHNOLOGY: one of a variety of documents across a range of media that humans have invented and in turn used to archive and disseminate ideas, beliefs, stories, and other evidence of production.

Ownership and use of printing presses and access to (or restriction of) information/materials, libraries, and archives has long been a site of struggle, related in many ways to revolutionary activity and the fight for civil rights and free speech all over the world. While (in many countries) the contemporary quotidian landscape has indeed drastically shifted in its access to platforms for sharing information and in the widespread ability to "publish" digitally, even with extremely limited resources, the importance of publication on physical media has not diminished. In fact, this may be the most critical time in recent history for activist groups, artists, and others to insist upon learning, establishing, and encouraging personal and community documentation practices.

With The OS's print endeavors I wanted to open up a conversation about this: the ultimately radical, transgressive act of creating PRINT / DOCUMENTATION in the digital age. It's a question of the archive, and of history: who gets to tell the story, and what evidence of our lives, our behaviors, and/or our experiences are we leaving behind? We can know little to nothing about the future into which we're leaving an unprecedentedly digital document trail--but we can be assured that publications, government agencies, museums, schools, and other institutional powers that be will continue to leave BOTH a digital and print version of their production for the official record. Will we?

As a (rogue) anthropologist and long time academic, I can easily pull up many accounts about how lives, behaviors, experiences--how THE STORY of a time or place--was pieced together using the deep study of the archive: correspondence, notebooks, and other physical documents which are no longer the norm in many lives and practices. As we move our creative behaviors towards digital note taking, and even audio and video, what can we predict about future technology that is in any way assuring that our stories will be accurately told--or told at all? How will we leave these things for the record?

For all our years of print publication, I've said that "with these documents we say: WE WERE HERE, WE EXISTED, WE HAVE A DIFFERENT STORY", but now, with the rapid expansion of greater volume with digital and DIY printed media, we add: we ARE here, and while we are, we will not be limited in what we add value to, share, make accessible, or give voice to, by restricting it to what we can afford to print in volume.

Adding a digital series is the next chapter of *our* story: a way for us to support more creative practitioners and offer folks independent options for POD or DIY-zine-style distribution, even without our financial means changing -- which means, each book will *also* have archive-ready print manifestations. It's our way of challenging what is required to evolve and grow. Ever onward, outward, beyond.

Elæ [Lynne DeSilva-Johnson]. Founder& Creative Director
THE OPERATING SYSTEM, Brooklyn NY 2019

THE 2019 OS CHAPBOOK SERIES

DIGITAL TITLES:

American Policy Player's Guide and Dream Book - Rachel Zolf
The George Oppen Memorial BBQ - Eric Benick
Flight Of The Mothman - Gyasi Hall
Mass Transitions - Sue Landers
Music Of Each Slain Creature - Frank Sherlock
The Grass Is Greener When The Sun Is Yellow - Sarah Rosenthal & Valerie Witte
From Being Things, To Equalities In All - Joe Milazzo
These Deals Won't Last Forever - Sasha Amari Hawkins
Ventriloquy - Bonnie Emerick
A Period Of Non-Enforcement - Lindsay Miles
Quantum Mechanics : Memoirs Of A Quark - Brad Baumgartner
Hara-Kiri On Monkey Bars - Anna Hoff

✳✳✳

PRINT TITLES:

Vela. - Knar Gavin
[零] A Phantom Zero - Ryu Ando
Don't Be Scared - Magdalena Zurawski
Re: Verses - Kristina Darling & Chris Campanioni

✳✳✳

PLEASE SEE OUR FULL CATALOG
FOR FULL LENGTH VOLUMES AND PREVIOUS CHAPBOOK SERIES:
HTTPS://SQUAREUP.COM/STORE/THE-OPERATING-SYSTEM/

DOC U MENT
/däkyəmənt/

First meant "instruction" or "evidence," whether written or not.

noun - a piece of written, printed, or electronic matter that provides information or evidence or that serves as an official record
verb - record (something) in written, photographic, or other form
synonyms - paper - deed - record - writing - act - instrument

[Middle English, precept, from Old French, from Latin *documentum*, example, proof, from *docre*, to teach; see *dek-* in Indo-European roots.]

Who is responsible for the manufacture of value?

Based on what supercilious ontology have we landed in a space where we vie against other creative people in vain pursuit of the fleeting credibilities of the scarcity economy, rather than freely collaborating and sharing openly with each other in ecstatic celebration of MAKING?

While we understand and acknowledge the economic pressures and fear-mongering that threatens to dominate and crush the creative impulse, we also believe that *now more than ever we have the tools to relinquish agency via cooperative means,* fueled by the fires of the Open Source Movement.

Looking out across the invisible vistas of that rhizomatic parallel country we can begin to see our community beyond constraints, in the place where intention meets resilient, proactive, collaborative organization.

Here is a document born of that belief, sown purely of imagination and will. When we document we assert. We print to make real, to reify our being there. When we do so with mindful intention to address our process, to open our work to others, to create beauty in words in space, to respect and acknowledge the strength of the page we now hold physical, a thing in our hand… we remind ourselves that, like Dorothy: *we had the power all along, my dears.*

THE PRINT! DOCUMENT SERIES
is a project of
the trouble with bartleby
in collaboration with
the operating system

www.ingramcontent.com/pod-product-compliance
Lightning Source LLC
Chambersburg PA
CBHW030349100526
44592CB00010B/888